SPACE

D1486123

PLANETS NEAR EARTH

Ian Graham

W
FRANKLIN WATTS
LONDON•SYDNEY

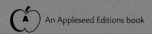

An Appleseed Editions book

First published in Great Britain in 2016
by The Watts Publishing Group

Designed by Guy Callaby
Edited by Mary-Jane Wilkins

Picture acknowledgements
t = top, b = bottom, l = left,
r = right, c = centre
title page Computer Earth; 2-3 Johan
Swanepoel; 4 Aaron Rutten; 5 Katharina
Wittfeld/all Shutterstock; 6 Digital Vision/
Thinkstock; 7tr Terrance Emerson/
Shutterstock, c Digital Vision/Thinkstock;
8 NASA/JPL/USGS; Elenarts; 10 leonello
calvetti; 11 Zyankarlo/all Shutterstock;
12 © Andrea Danti; 13 JulienGrondin;
14 Purestock; 15 Stocktrek Images/all
Thinkstock; 16t and b NASA/JPL-Caltech/
MSSS; 17 Getty Images; 18 Photodisc/
all Thinkstock; 19 artwork Guy Callaby/
NASA/John Hopkins University Applied
Physics Laboratory/Carnegie Institute
of Washington; 20 NASA/JPL-Caltech;
21 Stocktrek Images
Cover t to b: Tristan3D/Shutterstock,
Digital Vision/Thinkstock, Marcel Clemens/
Shutterstock, Tristan3D/Thinkstock

Dewey number 523.4
HB ISBN 978 1 4451 4918 9

Printed in China

Franklin Watts
An imprint of
Hachette Children's Group
Part of The Watts Publishing Group
Carmelite House
50 Victoria Embankment
London EC4Y 0DZ

An Hachette UK Company
www.hachette.co.uk

www.franklinwatts.co.uk

CONTENTS

When the near planets formed, they were so hot that they melted. Over millions of years, the heat slowly escaped into space. As they cooled, their surface hardened into a rocky crust.

Earth

Mars

Venus

Mercury

The near planets are also called terrestrial planets, meaning that they are like Earth.

SURROUNDED BY GAS

The near planets are surrounded by a mixture of gases called an atmosphere. Mercury and Mars have very thin atmospheres. Earth is surrounded by air. Venus has the thickest atmosphere.

Earth is surrounded by a blanket of air speckled with white clouds.

FEW MOONS

The eight planets of the solar system have more than 160 moons, but only three orbit the near planets. Mercury and Venus have no moons, Earth has one and Mars has two.

SPOTLIGHT ON SPACE

VENUS

Venus is the planet closest to Earth and it's nearly the same size as Earth. But these twin planets are very different from each other.

HOTHOUSE WORLD

The surface of Venus is hidden under a very thick poisonous atmosphere. The atmosphere traps heat from the Sun, making Venus the hottest planet in the solar system.

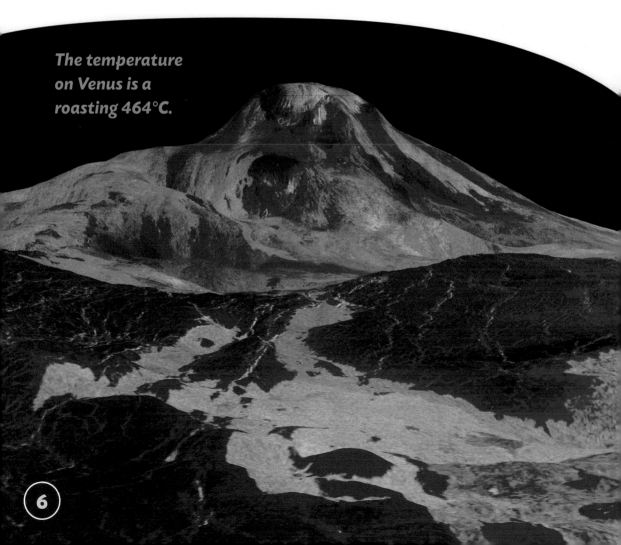

The temperature on Venus is a roasting 464°C.

BACKWARD SPIN

When the planets formed, they were all spinning in the same direction. Today, Venus spins in the opposite direction. No one knows what made Venus change direction.

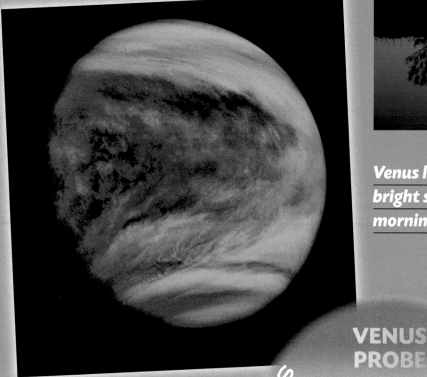

Venus looks like a bright star in the morning or evening.

Venus's atmosphere is mostly carbon dioxide with sulphuric acid clouds!

VENUS PROBE

The surface of Venus was seen for the first time in 1975 when a spacecraft called Venera 9 landed on the planet. Its pictures showed ground covered with small rocks.

SPOTLIGHT ON SPACE

EXPLORING VENUS

Venus has been studied by spacecraft that were able to look through its thick clouds and see the planet's surface.

SEEING VENUS

The *Magellan* and *Pioneer Venus* spacecraft fired radio waves through Venus's clouds. The waves bounced back, which helped the spacecraft to work out the shape of Venus's surface.

The colours in this map of Venus show ground of different height.

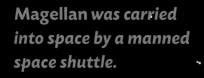
Magellan was carried into space by a manned space shuttle.

MAGELLAN

To save money, the *Magellan* spacecraft was built from spare parts left over from other spacecraft. *Magellan* spent four years orbiting Venus and studying it.

REVEALING VENUS

Spacecraft including **Pioneer Venus, Magellan** *and* **Venus Express** *have discovered what Venus is like. Under poisonous clouds, it has hundreds of volcanoes, many more than Earth has.*

SPOTLIGHT ON SPACE

EARTH

The third planet from the Sun is our home in space. Earth is the only planet in the whole Universe where we know life exists.

WATER WORLD

Earth is a watery world. It is exactly the right distance from the Sun for water to be liquid. And life is found everywhere on Earth where there is water.

Most of Earth's surface is covered with water.

THE MOON

Earth has one moon, the Moon. It's one of the biggest moons in the solar system. Apart from Earth, it is the only world that people have set foot on.

THE SEASONS

Earth has seasons because it tilts or leans over. The part that tilts towards the Sun is warmer – here it's summer. Six months later, this part tilts away from the Sun and it's winter there.

SPOTLIGHT ON SPACE

The same side of the Moon is always turned towards Earth.

INSIDE EARTH

Earth is not the same all the way through.
When it formed, the heaviest substances sank
to its centre and the lightest floated on top.

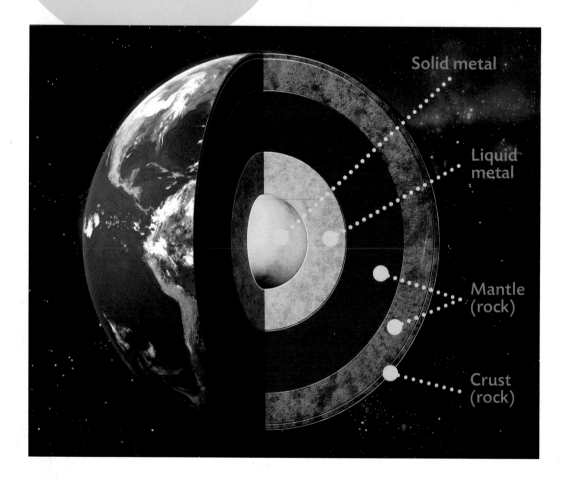

Solid metal

Liquid metal

Mantle (rock)

Crust (rock)

METAL CORE

At the centre of the Earth there is a
big ball of hot metal. Some of it is liquid.
The rest of the Earth is made of rock.

*Earth's core is as hot
as the Sun's surface.*

BROKEN CRUST

Earth's surface is constantly moving. Its crust is broken into pieces like a cracked eggshell. The pieces move very slowly. The edges rub against each other and push into each other.

EARTH'S WEATHER

Earth's surface never stops changing. Wind, rain, tides, storms, landslides, volcanoes and earthquakes reshape the land. Over millions of years, coastlines have changed and whole islands and mountains have appeared or disappeared.

SPOTLIGHT ON SPACE

Volcanoes are common where plates of the Earth's crust rub against each other.

MARS

Mars, the red planet, is a bit like Earth. It has seasons like Earth's and it also has ice caps at its poles.

SEARCHING FOR WATER

Mars is dry today, but did it have water in the past? Spacecraft have searched for clues and they have found signs that Mars was a wet world like Earth in the past.

The Mars Reconnaissance Orbiter spacecraft spotted rock that usually forms in water.

Olympus Mons last erupted about two million years ago.

MEGA-VOLCANO

The biggest volcano in the whole solar system is Olympus Mons on Mars. It's nearly three times higher than the highest mountain on Earth.

MARTIAN MOONS

Mars has two tiny moons, called Phobos and Deimos. Deimos rises in the east, just like Earth's Moon, but Phobos rises in the west and crosses the sky in the opposite direction.

SPOTLIGHT ON SPACE

EXPLORING MARS

Spacecraft have been exploring Mars since the 1960s. The *Curiosity* rover is the latest robot explorer to land on the planet.

A CURIOUS ROBOT

Curiosity landed on Mars on 6 August 2012. It's a nuclear-powered vehicle about the size of a small car. *Curiosity* is the fourth rover to land on Mars.

*The **Curiosity** rover on Mars is steered by drivers on Earth.*

MARTIAN CANALS

In the 1800s, some astronomers thought they saw straight lines on Mars. They thought the lines were canals built by Martians. But when the first spacecraft arrived, there were no canals or Martians.

LIFE ON MARS?

In 1996, scientists found tiny worm-like features inside a rock from Mars that had landed on Earth. Was it Martian life? Some scientists thought it was, but others did not agree.

SPOTLIGHT ON SPACE

Astronomers made maps of canals on Mars, but the canals weren't there at all.

Mercury

Mercury is the smallest of the near planets and the closest to the Sun. It is not much bigger than the Moon and looks similar to it.

Hot and cold

The side of Mercury that faces the Sun is roasted at four times the temperature of boiling water. The dark side of Mercury plunges to a bone-chilling -200°C.

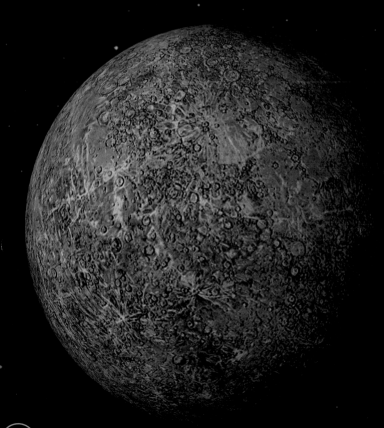

The sunlit side of Mercury is hot enough to melt tin!

INSIDE MERCURY

If you could slice Mercury open, you'd find a big ball of iron inside. This metal core is surrounded by rock called the mantle, with a thin crust of lighter rock on top.

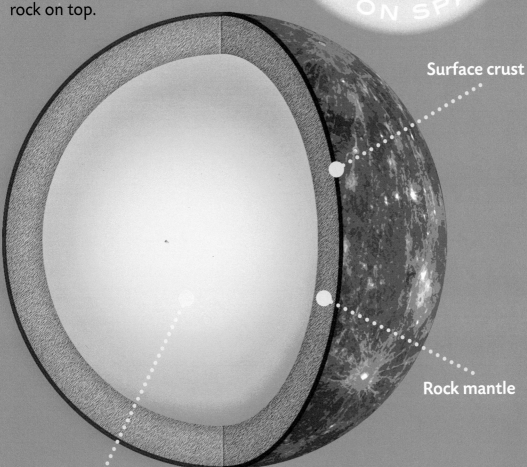

Surface crust

Rock mantle

Huge metal core

Mercury has a very big metal core for such a small planet.

EXPLORING MERCURY

Mercury is very hard to explore because it is so close to the Sun. Spacecraft visiting Mercury have to work in the Sun's scorching heat. Only two spacecraft have visited.

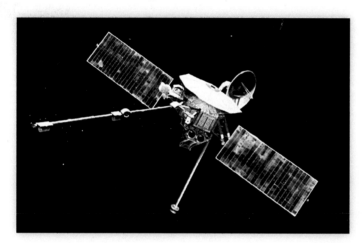

MARINER 10

After taking the first close-up photographs of Venus, *Mariner 10* moved on to fly past Mercury. Then it looped round the Sun and flew past Mercury twice more.

Mariner 10 took about 7,000 photographs of Mercury and Venus.

MESSENGER TO MERCURY

A space probe called *Messenger* became the second spacecraft to visit Mercury in 2008. After flying past the tiny planet three times, it went into orbit around Mercury.

AN ICY SURPRISE

One of Messenger's most surprising discoveries is that there is ice on Mercury. Craters at Mercury's north pole are always in shadow and so are cold enough for ice to form.

SPOTLIGHT ON SPACE

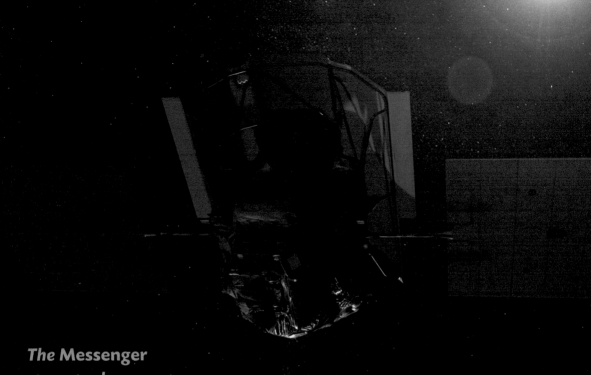

The Messenger space probe took 100,000 photographs of Mercury.

GLOSSARY

astronomer A scientist who studies the Universe beyond Earth.

atmosphere The gases that surround a star, planet or moon.

carbon dioxide A gas found in the atmosphere of some planets including Earth, Venus and Mars.

core The centre of a planet or moon.

crater A shallow hole on the surface of a planet or moon, caused by a piece of rock hitting the surface, or by a volcano erupting.

crust The surface of a planet like Earth, made of rock.

fault A crack in the Earth's surface where two or more plates of the Earth's crust meet.

ice cap Ice that spreads out in all directions, especially on top of a mountain or at the poles of a planet or moon.

mantle The part of a planet between the core and the crust.

moon A small world that orbits another body, such as a planet.

nuclear-powered Powered by atoms (particles of matter) breaking down and producing heat that can be used to make electricity.

planet A large world in orbit around the Sun or another star.

reconnaissance Exploration to collect information.

rover A vehicle sent to explore a planet or moon that uses instruments to study the surface and atmosphere.

solar system The Sun and all the planets, moons and other bodies that travel through space with it.

space probe An unmanned spacecraft sent from Earth to explore planets, moons and other bodies.

space shuttle A manned spacecraft used again and again. NASA had a fleet of up to five shuttles that made 135 flights between 1981 and 2011.

sulphuric acid A chemical substance found in the atmosphere of Venus.

terrestrial planet A planet that is like Earth: made of rock with a metal core.

Universe Everything that is known to exist – all the stars, planets, moons and everything else.

WEBSITES

http://mars.jpl.nasa.gov/participate/funzone/
Games and activities linked to Mars from the space agency NASA.

http://solarsystem.nasa.gov/kids/models/MESSENGER_Model.pdf
Make your own model of the *Messenger* space probe that was sent to explore Mercury.

http://www.kidsastronomy.com/mercury.htm
Find out how much you would weigh on Mercury and why it has no atmosphere.

http://scienceforkids.kidipede.com/physics/space/venus.htm
Find out how long a day is on Venus and why you couldn't live there.

http://www.kidsgeo.com/geography-for-kids/0001-hello-earth.php
Lots of information about Earth and what we know about it.

http://www.kidsastronomy.com/mars_explorer.htm
Read about the many spacecraft and rovers that have explored Mars.

http://www.youtube.com/watch?v=P4boyXQuUlw
This video shows you how the *Curiosity* rover landed on Mars and what it did then.

INDEX